Unlocking Interceptions

Helen Adams Garrett

Copyright 1997 by Helen Adams Garrett
All rights reserved.

No part of this book may be reproduced or transmitted in any form or by any means, electronic or mechanical, including photocopying or recording, or by any information storage and retrieval system, without written permission from the author and publisher. Requests and inquiries may be mailed to: American Federation of Astrologers, 6535 S. Rural Road, Tempe AZ 85283.

ISBN-10: 0-86690-533-2
ISBN-13: 978-0-86690-533-6

First Printing: 1997
Current Printing: 2011

Published by:
American Federation of Astrologers, Inc.
6535 S. Rural Road
Tempe AZ 85283.

Printed in the United States of America

Contents

Different House Systems	1
Interceptions Through the Houses	9
First/Seventh Houses	13
Second/Eighth Houses	19
Third/Ninth Houses	25
Fourth/Tenth Houses	31
Fifth/Eleventh Houses	39
Sixth/Twelfth Houses	45
Multiple Interceptions	53
Ten Signs Intercepted in Two Houses	59
More on Interceptions	65
Summary of Interpretation Method	73

Different House Systems

Questions concerning interceptions have confounded practically every astrology teacher at some time and perhaps a large number in prior centuries since 200 B.C. We are still trying to perceive Ptolemy's reference to chart divisions.

Most anyone in North America will use Placidus, Koch, equal house or the Hamburg system. Regiomontanus, also known as the rational house system, is widely used in Europe. Selection of the house system can be of ultimate importance when examining interceptions. As James H. Holden said of several systems in his forward to Emma Belle Donath's *Houses: Which And When,* "it fails in polar latitudes."

Alcabitius was introduced by a Greek astrologer in the fifth century. He trisected the arc from the Ascendant to the Midheaven. This arc was equal to the semidiurnal arc of the Ascendant degree (whatever that means!). It required tables to calculate. It must have caught an eye since the Arabs kept it going for about 700 years.

Campanus came to us by way of Campano of Italy in the thirteenth century. There is no way I can explain the logic of this system without copying someone else's work. It is highly honored by scientific and mathematical astrologers and you can read about it in Emma Belle Donath's book mentioned above. It works well at higher latitudes.

Equal house is a very early system known to Ptolemy. It puts the degree of the Ascendant on the first house cusp and the same degree on each cusp of the succeeding signs around the chart.

Koch, also called birthplace, was introduced in a book in 1960 by Walter Koch. His idea was to make a system more perfect than Regiomontanus and Placidus. He worked from a misconception, however, and did not succeed with any more exactness to the birthplace and "it fails in the polar regions."

The Meridian house system was developed by David Cope of Australia in the early 1900s. It is an adaptation of the Morinus system and is calculated from the Midheaven and reaches to the poles.

Morinus is a product of Jean Baptiste Morin, a medical doctor and professor of mathematics around 1630 in Paris. He was an advocate of Regiomontanus and devised his system to work all the way to the poles. He calculated the cusps not from the Ascendant but from the Midheaven.

Placidus by Placidus de Titis (1603-1668) was a result of his attempt to decipher Ptolemy's system and publish what he thought Ptolemy had in mind. What he had extracted correctly was primary direction. However, like all quadrant systems (calculated from the Ascendant) "it fails in the polar latitudes" beyond 66N32.

Porphyry is a modification of the Equal house system and attempts to divide the quadrants of the horoscope in a more equal manner. Both the Ascendant and the Midheaven are calculated, and the "equal" is based on the degrees between the two. The system dates back to the second century.

Regiomontanus, or the rational house system, works well above 66N32 or 66S32 latitude and in any other location. Johann Muller (1436-1476), a Bavarian astrologer known as Regiomontanus, studied Ptolemy's works. His conclusions for calculating house cusps were the first tables of houses printed. The system reigned for 200 years. It went down with astrology during the Middle Ages but is making a comeback because of its now recognized and accepted accuracy.

Solar houses place the degree of the Sun on the Ascendant and the same degree on each sign/cusp of the remaining houses, all houses being equal. (I use this system when a birth time is unavailable except I place zero degrees of the Sun sign on the first house cusp.) There are no interceptions in any equal house chart.

Most house systems that are derived from the Ascendant will agree on the Ascendant and Midheaven. A house system derived from the Midheaven may or may not agree with any other house system, mostly because the tenth house cusp will not be the same as the Midheaven.

Different house systems present various ranges of interception. We offer you some of the results of Rudy Flack's research on the technicalities and allow you to make some decisions of your own. Since most North Americans use Placidus for natal charts, most of the examples for interpretation will be based on the Placidus house system. The method of the interpretation technique should be applicable in all systems. It is necessary to use Regiomontanus (or Campanus or Morinus) for charts beyond 66N32 or 66S32 latitude.

Interception/House System Facts

1. When you use a house system that is developed from the Ascendant, such as Placidus or Koch, it will not calculate a correct chart above 60N or 60S latitude.

2. In house systems that are derived from the poles, such as Regiomontanus and Campanus, the Midheaven is calculated first. These systems will thus yield a proper chart all the way from the equator to the poles.

3. Equal house or solar-sign houses will not show any interceptions.

4. You can have an interception anywhere on the surface of the earth, from the equator to the poles.

5. On the shortest day in the northern hemisphere there are no interceptions at midnight. The maximum number are at noon with a proportional number in-between. The reverse is the case in the southern hemisphere.

6. On the longest day in the northern hemisphere there are no interceptions at noon. The maximum number are at midnight with a proportional number in between. The reverse is the case in the southern hemisphere.

7. When viewing a chart represented with proportional house spacing, the Midheaven will point directly to the top of

the chart at the equinoxes, but at the solstices the Midheaven will be skewed over toward the eastern horizon (near the summer solstice) or toward the western horizon (near the winter solstice).

8. At the poles you can have up to five sets of interceptions and the Ascendant and Midheaven can be conjunct, opposite, at a ninety-degree angle from each other or somewhere in between; it is dependent upon the date used.

9. When analyzing a chart cast for a point above 66N32 in the northern hemisphere, during the course of a one year period of time the Ascendant will travel across half of the zodiac (Capricorn through Cancer) in six and a half hours, spending only three minutes in Pisces. The Ascendant crosses the remainder of the zodiac (Leo through Sagittarius) during the remaining approximate 364 days.

10. In the northern hemisphere, interceptions are more frequent between the autumnal equinox and spring equinox, and less frequent from the spring equinox to the autumnal equinox.

11. Typically there are more interceptions at the higher latitudes and fewer at the lower latitudes.

12. At any given latitude or longitude, interceptions can vary from none to one or more, based on the time of the day.

Interceptions: Where and When

We have not thus far been able to calculate the percentage of potential for interceptions to appear, but an estimate is a probable fifty-fifty.

Beginning at about 43N, from 0 Scorpio to 0 Pisces, there is potential for two sets of interceptions. From about 58N in a few degrees of Scorpio and Aquarius there is a potential for three sets of interceptions. From 60N latitude to 90N latitude (the poles), it will finally reach a point where all but two to four signs can be intercepted. At this point Pisces may be on the Ascendant for only three minutes because Virgo is only three minutes on the Descendant.

If you are going there for a honeymoon it may be a good idea to take a double sleeping bag for an ideal Pisces moment. Otherwise there won't be time to walk across an igloo before the moment is gone. By the same token, the Ascendant may be short but the nights are long.

If you go in summer, you may not need sleeping bags as it is almost always daytime. That's a tough assignment for a night person.

There are times at every place on Earth when there are no interceptions at all, even at the poles. At the more northern latitudes this occurs near noon in the summer months. There are also interceptions at the equator but very sparse, from 0N and 0S through 15N and 15S latitude.

Without calculating a chart we cannot guess whether there are any interceptions. As indicated in the fact list, interceptions are more frequent between the autumnal equinox and spring equinox, and less frequent from the spring equinox to the autumnal equinox.

It may be worthy to mention that I have prepared charts for numerous clients who were born in India and the Orient.

Since it is easier to apply interpretations to people we know, I looked back at chart after chart and found that I did not have a single person with an interception who was born in India, China or Japan. About one-third of China and most all of India are south of the Gulf of Mexico's northern coastline of the southern United States, roughly 30N latitude.

Interceptions vary in the different house systems. For example, a chart in one system may have a set of interceptions in the third and ninth houses, while the same identical data using a different system may render different signs intercepted in the fourth and tenth houses.

It is suggested that you consider the application by interpretation and use whichever best suits your life events. You might decide to ignore interceptions completely and go with an equal house system which has the same degree on all house cusps and no interceptions. There are always duplicated indications of any promise from the chart, and if the interceptions are not there, the planets will impart the message in some form or fashion. Interceptions just display more detail.

Interceptions Through the Houses

First, we define interception. Imagine for a moment that you are at a football game. A player passes the ball to another teammate and someone runs between the two and takes the ball away from them. That is called an interception. The dictionary says: "verb 1) to stop or interrupt the progress or course of, 2) prevent, hinder, 3) to interrupt communication or connection with, 4) intersect." Interception, the noun, is the subject of any of these actions.

There is no indication that an interception is forever. It is only interrupted or taken away for a while after the team lost its ball to the other team. We have to wait for the proper time to earn the right for what the interceptions represents. Interceptions *are* karmic.

Many people are able to recognize the time when interceptions are opened by progression and when planets by transit put certain qualities of life in abeyance temporarily or release restrictions appropriate to the interceptions.

Analyze only one house holding an interception at a given time and note the degree on the cusp of that house to see how many degrees are left for time and planets to travel from the house cusp to the sign intercepted. For instance, a twenty-six degree Aquarius Ascendant has about three degrees left in the sign before reaching Pisces intercepted in the first house. If the birth time is correct, at age three the individual would experience an event signifying a life change applicable to the sign and its ruler or the planet which is approaching.

Capricorn on the Ascendant might have restricted the child during the three-year period of time due to an illness or because of some family limitation. A change would occur at about age three, bringing more social life and freedom as the chart progresses to Aquarius, the intercepted sign. When the Ascendant progresses through Aquarius in approximately thirty years, near age thirty-three, there would be another change. This time Pisces would be the governing influence. Some explicit examples will be shown later.

There are two major considerations when interpreting interceptions: the signs that are captured between other signs (in the intercepted houses), and the signs that occupy two or more house cusps which we refer to as duplicated signs.

Intercepted Signs

Because there are more interceptions at certain times of the year, some signs are more prone to be caught up in interceptions than others; but all signs are at some time intercepted.

- In order to know what is locked into the interception you need to identify the department of life it touches. What house holds it?
- What sign is intercepted? This tells what is missing.

- Where is the ruler of the intercepted sign? This should tell something of who or what intercepted you.

Duplicated Signs

When signs are missing by interception, other signs must occupy the other house cusps that were vacated. We call these duplicated signs. They are the keys that will help you unlock your treasures. It is as if you have a safety box or a vault with something of value in it. You also have the key and can go into the box. But you might want to wait for the bank to open or for what you consider an appropriate time to take out the treasures. If the ruler of your duplicated house is locked in the interception, you might have to wait longer or "borrow" a key by transit and use the energy of the ruler of your duplicated sign when it comes by the door to your interception.

We do not have just one interception. As they come in sets, you will have at least two. This means you will also have at least two sets of duplicated signs. Sometimes the ruler of one set of duplicates will automatically unlock both sets of interceptions.

- Look for the duplicated signs. Then find the rulers. Are they outside of the intercepted sign? They usually will be. Is it in the same house with the interception? This is like locking a door and leaving the key nearby. Just take it from under the door mat and open it up.
- If the ruler of the duplicated sign is in its own sign, you have an easy route to free the interception. Not only is the planet in its dignity, but transits of that sign provide longer terms to take advantage of the vibrations.
- If the ruler of the duplicated sign is in any other sign,

analyze it by house, sign and aspect, and use it in its best form to assist you.

As we go through the houses with interceptions you will see that interceptions do not deny production from the house represented. They simply indicate that one must earn the right to have the full benefits of whatever those signs represent. Sometimes the keys to unlock interceptions are locked within the intercepted sign or signs; in this case, the lock must be broken or a key borrowed from some other source. We have seen some charts that appear not to have been opened during their lifetime. These seem to occur with people who are confined for life or in the chart of someone who could not face the struggles of life and died from an early cause or committed suicide. Most of us will get gratification on some level from the interceptions and will come to a point that we hardly realize that we missed anything.

First/Seventh Houses

Interceptions in these houses indicate that the native makes a change in life corresponding with the age represented by the number of degrees difference from the Ascendant to the entry into the intercepted sign.

These houses could imply cooperation or competition. They could also prevent pleasant or unfulfilled contacts with others, both in childhood and in early adult life. These interceptions do open at some point during the life.

Alexander Graham Bell

Alexander Graham Bell's father taught deaf-mutes, thus stimulating his son's interest at an early age so that he studied music, elocution, physiology of speech and acoustics. Alexander had 15 Pisces on the natal Ascendant. At age fifteen, his Ascendant progressed to 0 Aries and he entered the University of Edinburgh.

The rulers of the duplicated signs, Mercury and Jupiter, are the opening keys to the interceptions of Aries and Libra. Bell had Mercury in Pisces and Jupiter in Gemini. We can readily see his willingness to help (Jupiter) other people (Aries/Libra) who were less fortunate (Virgo/Pisces).

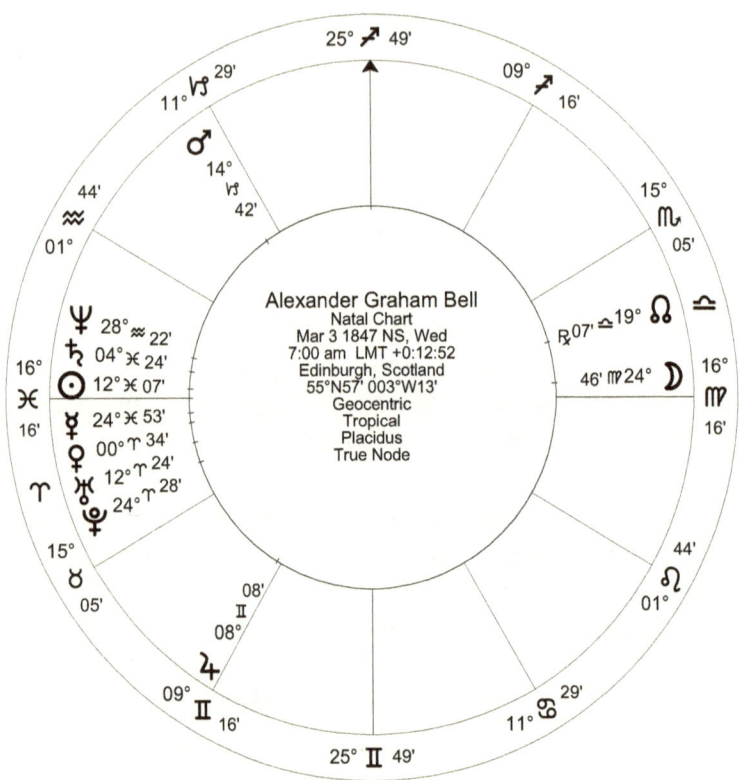

On March 10, 1876 Bell and his employee heard the first message transmitted by telephone. His diurnal Ascendant on that date was 13 Aries, one degree from his natal intercepted Uranus. Jupiter was entering Sagittarius, the sign duplicated on his ninth and tenth houses natally. He changed the way the world communicates.

An interesting note: Diurnal Venus (voice) was conjunct Neptune (artificial or facsimile). By progression, he had a

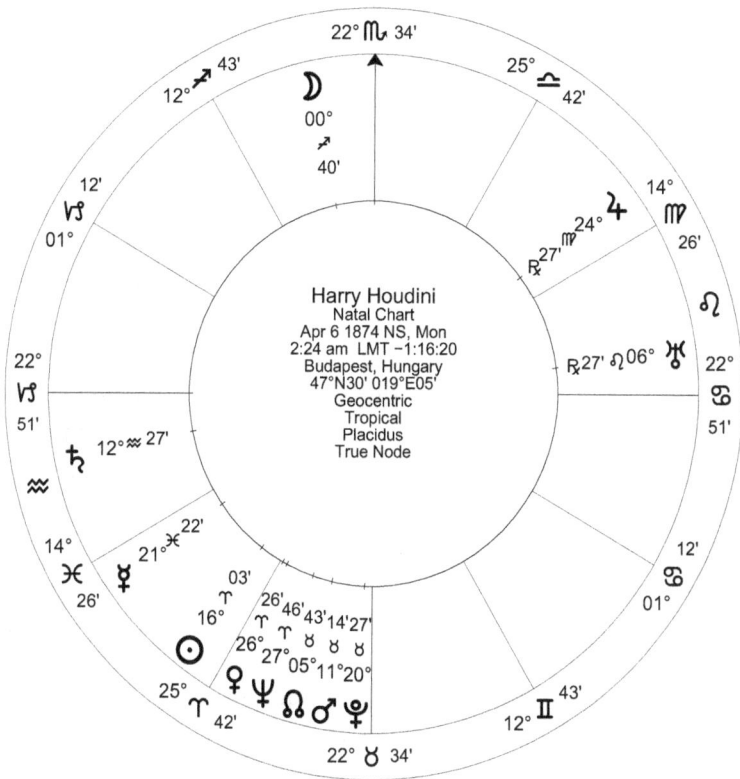

rare situation of both Aries and Taurus intercepted in the sixth house. The natal duplicated signs had progressed to his Ascendant and Descendant. Progressed Mercury and transiting Jupiter were conjunct his progressed Moon and natal Moon.

Harry Houdini

Harry Houdini, born Ehrich Weiss, had Aquarius and Leo intercepted in the first and seventh houses. The duplicated signs were Cancer on the sixth and seventh houses and Capricorn on the twelfth and first houses. The Moon and Saturn were the keys to open the delays and restrictions. Houdini was a world famous escape artist.

His Moon, elevated in the tenth house in Sagittarius, certainly supplies exciting and enjoyable activity to assist in unlocking his interceptions. This was successfully accomplished through the seventh house. Crowds anxiously awaited his performances wherever he made an appearance. As is typical of Saturn in the first house, he kept trying to prove himself better in each task. Saturn was his other key and it was locked up in the first house. He held to the desire to maintain the right to restrain himself (Saturn) and then free himself (Aquarius). He promised his wife that if he could, he would appear to her after death. It was never made public if he did.

Male Suicide

We immediately see some flags in this chart. Cause of death is self-undoing, ruler of the eighth in Aries. Venus at 0 Gemini loves two people at the same time because Venus in Gemini gets bored easily. No two loves would be alike. Venus is square Mars in Pisces, indicating the inability to limit deceptions. Mars trine Uranus in the seventh could keep a good supply of replacements, but Uranus inconjunct Venus loses control of the special one. All of this takes place outside of the interceptions, except that Venus rules Taurus intercepted in the first house and Mars co-rules Scorpio, intercepted in the seventh house.

How could the interceptions be opened? The keys are Mercury ruling the second and third and Jupiter ruling the eighth and ninth. Mercury represents communication and Ju-

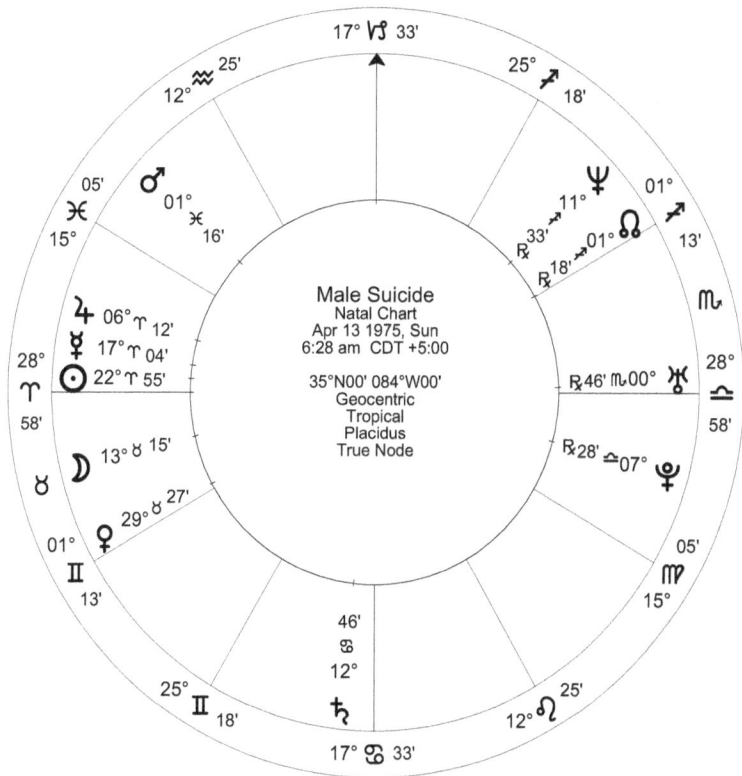

piter, especially because it rules the ninth, represents *truth*. Both Mercury and Jupiter are in Aries in the twelfth house. The negative side of truth—boasting—could have contributed to self-undoing.

The twenty-ninth degree of Aries lets us know he struggled for attention; it being on the Ascendant compounds the need. Pluto, ruler of the intercepted Scorpio, is in Libra, sign of partnerships, in the twelfth house to the seventh (the sixth) and is opposed by Jupiter. He no doubt found that special person cheating and could not overcome rejection because of low self-esteem. Chiron exactly conjunct the Sun says that from birth the individual needed to learn to live on a high spiritual plane and be prepared to adjust to any situation.

Second/Eighth Houses

Projects the focus on values of life, earning power and attitudes toward possessions and how we give and receive. There is emphasis on joint ventures, such as shared enterprises, insurance, taxes, inherited property, material goods entrusted to our care, intimacies (sexual participation) and moral issues that might contribute to emotional status.

Jack Nicklaus

Capricorn is intercepted in the second and Cancer in the eighth house in Nicklaus's chart. The duplicated signs, his keys, are Taurus on the sixth and Scorpio on the twelfth house. Anyone reviewing the financial success of professional golfers would not place Nicklaus at the top of the list.

What else would be expected with Capricorn intercepted in the second and Saturn in the fifth ruling play, fun and entertainment? So to what has he resorted?

Venus ruling the sixth and seventh houses is in Pisces in the third house. Selling is the correct answer in a sense, but Pisces suggests that he does not personally sell people. He sells "just because" he advertises. Both Pluto, ruler of Scorpio, and Scorpio's co-ruler, Mars, are in gambling houses (fifth and ninth). Mars certainly represents the first person

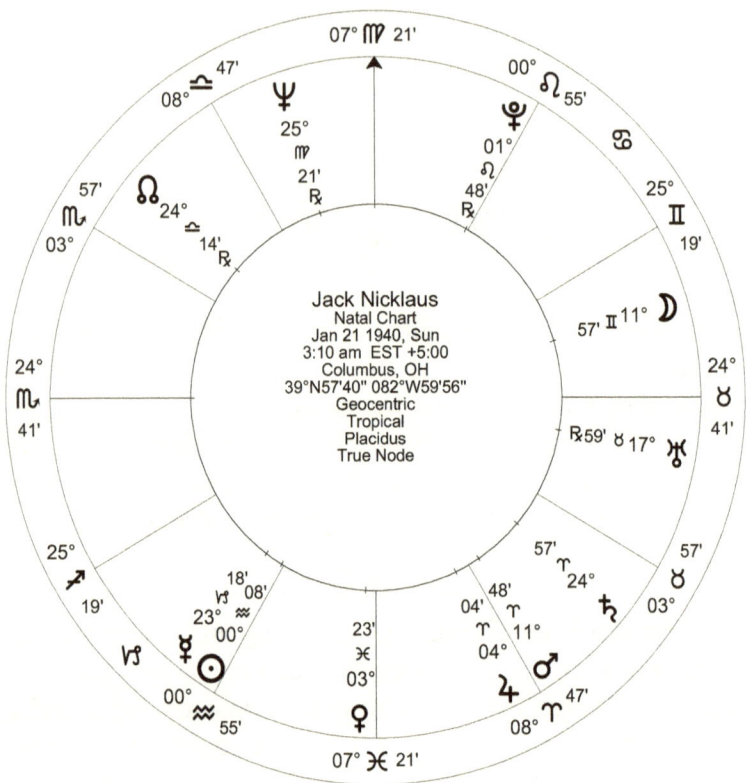

participation of play, but Pluto in the ninth confirms outdoor design that transforms scrub land into gorgeous greens.

In his 1962 solar return, Venus, which is one of his keys, was at 28 Capricorn in his second house interception, and the Moon was at 29 Cancer in the eighth house interception. Mars was in a progressed T-square from Aries. Pluto, the other key, sat right on the Midheaven and together they broke the lock. He was off to success!

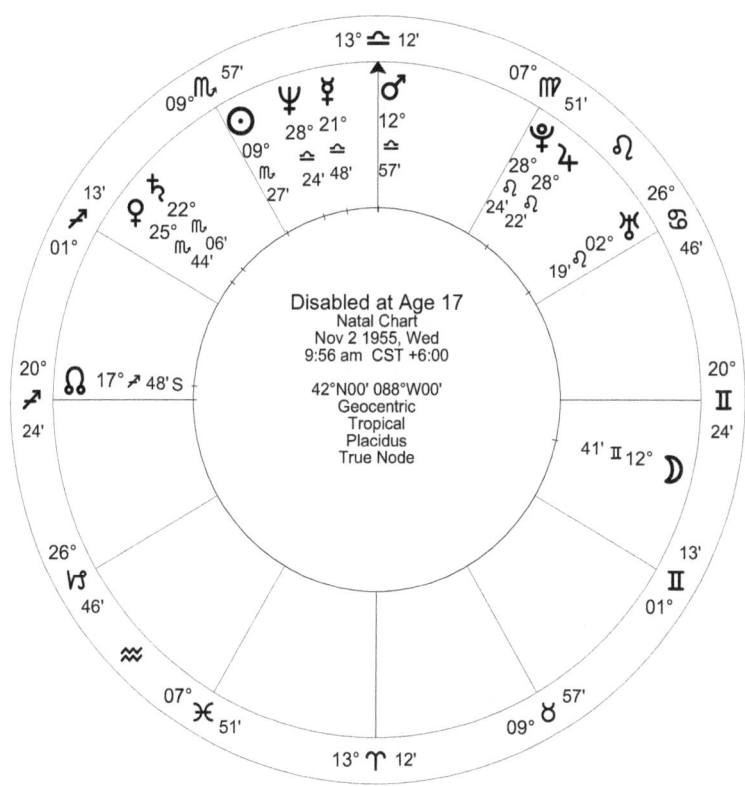

Disabled at Age 17

When we apply the 1972 solar return and progressions, we see some of what contributed to the disability. Aquarius and Leo are intercepted in the second and eighth houses. The eighth is packed with Uranus, which rules a higher vibration of the message and nerve system connected to the brain, in Leo, so these activities would relate strongly to personal pride. Jupiter rules hips/legs and blood, also in Leo. Pluto in Leo rules, among other things, muscles.

So we know from the beginning that there is a weakness that will affect the heart because Venus, ruler of the fifth house, is square Jupiter and Pluto, which rules Scorpio, the natural eighth house ruler (muscles). Mercury and Jupiter rule the duplicated signs on the sixth/seventh and twelfth/first, respectively. Mercury is in the tenth in Libra, so how he relates to his parents and their relationship could very well have a bearing on his health. Since Jupiter, the other duplicated ruler, is locked up, self-confidence and optimism must build and work from within the interception to break out. Jupiter in the eighth can reconstruct the body through sheer faith, to say nothing of the assistance from the greatest of all rebuilders, Pluto, being in its natural place in the eighth.

Eleanor Roosevelt

The Leo-Aquarius interception calls for a recognition of personal defects, which may be nothing more than having a misplaced talent for loving people who don't know how to return it. This can result in misery. When the duplicated signs are Taurus and Scorpio, it might call for taking a course in money handling or seduction, if sexual interest is low.

Her 1920 solar return held Chiron in the seventh, signifying that her husband would need adjustment. That summer he was stricken with polio. Solar return Pluto in the tenth house said she was to become very public. During the 1921 holiday season, Eleanor's progressed Moon conjunct her progressed Sun, both at 25 Scorpio in her natal eleventh house. The progressed New Moon in Scorpio gave her power, and she plunged headlong into a campaign to save her husband.

She had enjoyed an honorable reputation as an educator, but now became deeply involved in politics. Teddy Roose-

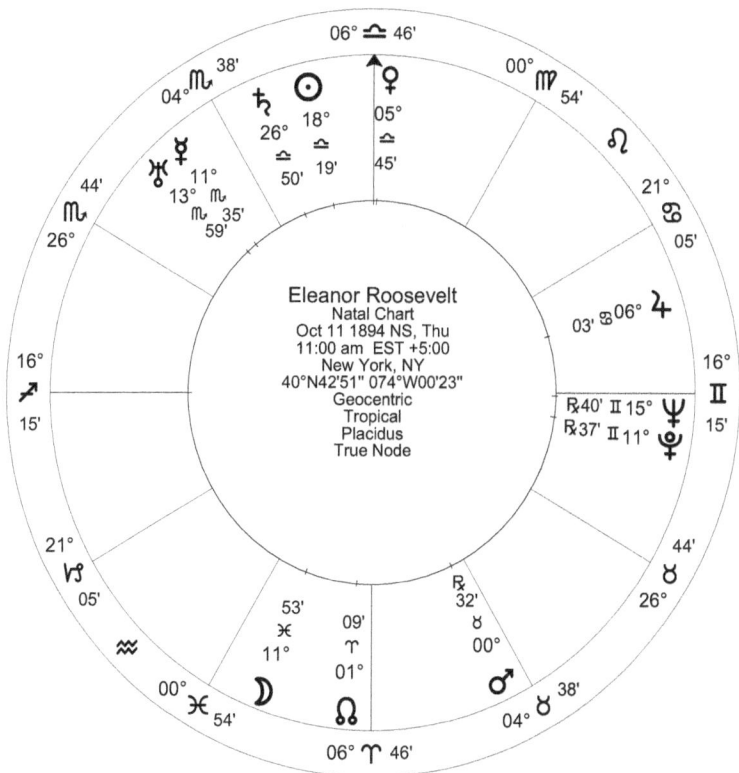

velt (the other party man) was her uncle. By 1924 she was financial chairman of the women's division of the New York State Commission, a post held until 1928. From there she held high office in state politics. She unlocked Aquarius through her political activities and when she turned the key, intercepted Jupiter, her natal ruler, was progressed conjunct her natal Venus, ruler of her other duplicated sign. Scorpio's co-ruler, Mars, was progressed conjunct her Ascendant.

Third/Ninth Houses

A third/ninth house interception relates to the need for guidance in compilation of rational thinking and education. Depending upon the signs, it could be very difficult to express deep emotional feelings. There could be speech and hearing malfunctions or learning disorders. Or, exceptional brilliance might not be well received by others.

Male Suicide 2

Capricorn and Cancer are the signs intercepted in the third house and ninth houses. Venus, ruler of the cause of death, is in the twelfth house of self-undoing in Libra. This is the first clue to the cause of death being attributed to the loss of a relationship. The second might be the duplicated signs Aries and Libra with Venus in Libra in the twelfth house and Mars intercepted in Capricorn in the third house. This could limit his thoughts as to what or how to express himself.

The Moon in Leo in the tenth can develop an attitude of "I deserve to be worshiped," and a tenth-house Moon has people-appeal. When Mars in Capricorn could not control and the Leo Moon was rejected, Venus, in the polite sign of Libra in the subconscious area of the twelfth house, shows there was insufficient confidence to survive the pain. It is sad that a young man with so much talent did not recognize his self-worth.

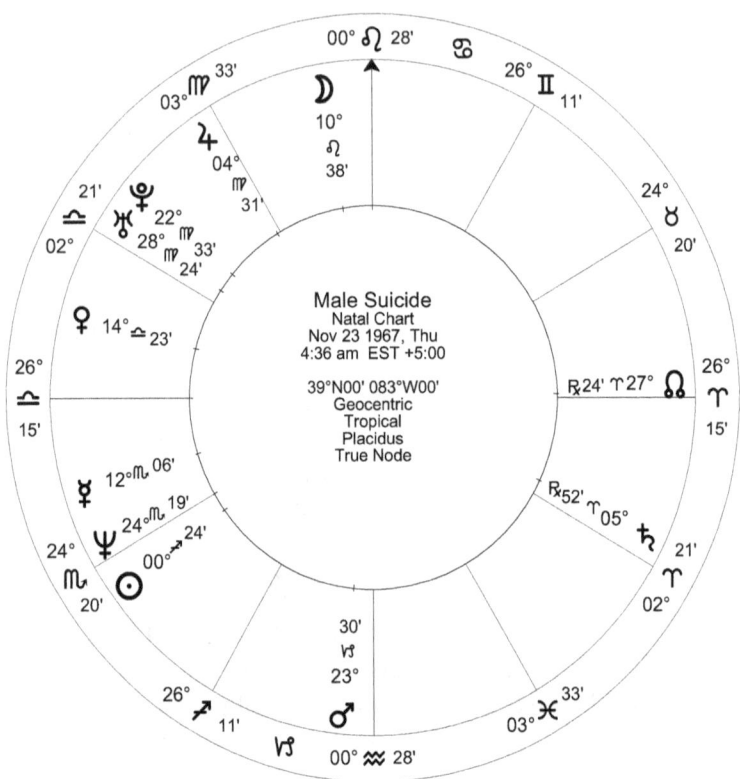

Helen Keller

Helen Keller's communication ability was closed when she was an infant as a result of a life-threatening illness that left her deaf and sightless. Leo and Aquarius are intercepted in her ninth and third houses. She experienced all the frustrations and confusions of difficult communication. She learned to speak, read and write, traveled widely and lectured on teaching deaf and blind students. She used a typewriter and could communicate in Greek. She maintained that the most

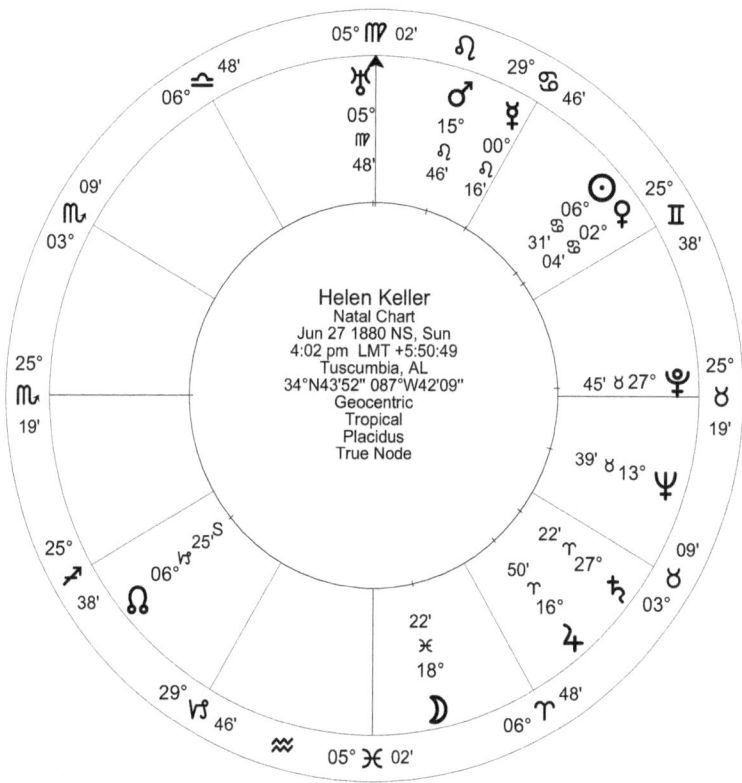

important day of her life was when she met her teacher, Anne Mansfield Sullivan.

Her duplicated signs were Taurus on the sixth and seventh houses and Scorpio on the twelfth and first houses. In her solar return when she met Miss Sullivan, Venus was conjunct transiting Neptune, both of which were conjunct her natal Pluto. This involved both keys to the duplicated houses. Mars, Scorpio's co-ruler, was transiting exactly trine solar return Mercury. Solar return Jupiter (education) and Venus were in the degree of the transiting Nodes, indicating a karmic venture.

Interestingly, she mentions in her *Story of my Life* that she had a great love for outdoor sports and studying religion, and that she had many far-off friends, all a party to her intercepted ninth house, which was opened to her through her Venus and Pluto contacts.

Allan Roy Dafoe, M.D.

Allan Dafoe had Mars at 29 Aries intercepted in the ninth house (he had severe scars on his face from a childhood accident). He was a medical doctor employed by a company that dismissed him when he was twenty-five. A licensed practitioner, there was an epidemic of diphtheria at the time and, although he saved many lives by administering antitoxins, he was fired because of their cost. His solar return that year had the Midheaven exactly trine Uranus in his natal chart in the second house, Virgo, which was one of his duplicated signs on the second and third houses. Solar return Mercury was exactly square 29 Virgo, the third house cusp, sending the message that he was to serve in his community.

Allan was a well-respected home-visit physician during the next twenty-six years. In his May 29, 1934 solar return, Uranus had moved from its natal second house, one of the duplicated sign houses, to the position of his natal Mars at 29 Aries, just two degrees shy of his Midheaven. If the interception had not been opened previously, it was now! Transiting Venus, which ruled Libra, the other intercepted sign, was conjunct Uranus and natal Mars. Solar return Jupiter, co-ruler of Pisces and ruler of the duplicated eighth and ninth

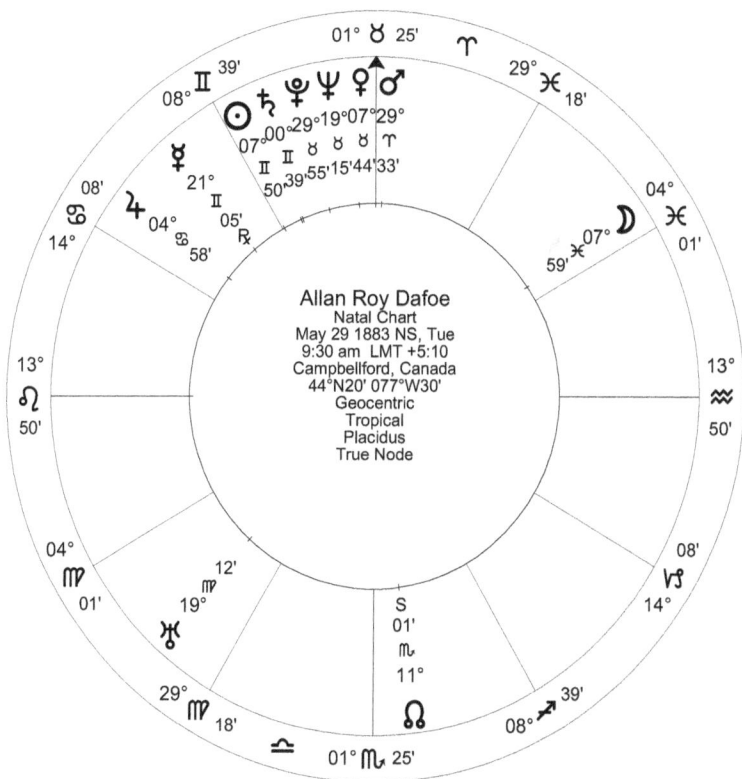

houses, was laughing like a court jester at the critical thirteenth degree of Libra in the intercepted third house because he now had to fight off the news media. Allan had, fewer than twenty-four hours earlier, delivered the Dionne quintuplets. Libra opened!

Fourth/Tenth Houses

The focus here is upon authority, both how one administers it and how one reacts to it. The fourth house represents the individual as a child and later as the head or co-head of the home. These houses express who we are in private and in public or the workplace. They indicate struggles, professional failures and successes, the image held by the public, home life, family members, and lifestyle.

Johnny Carson

Johnny Carson's chart has Aquarius and Leo intercepted in the fourth and tenth houses. Neptune in Leo in the tenth depicts a film-related career and possibly that what you see is not what you get. He also has the Nodes in the fourth and tenth houses at 29 Cancer/Capricorn, but not intercepted.

The appropriate keys to unlock the interceptions are Venus and Mars since Aries and Libra are the duplicated signs. It is almost as if Pluto stands guard at the top of the chart in the ninth house. His Moon in the critical thirteenth degree of a cardinal sign conjunct Jupiter lets him keep himself in hot water all the time. The other key is Venus is in Sagittarius, the sign of bachelors. Johnny, like a lot people with Venus in Sagittarius, did not want to marry.

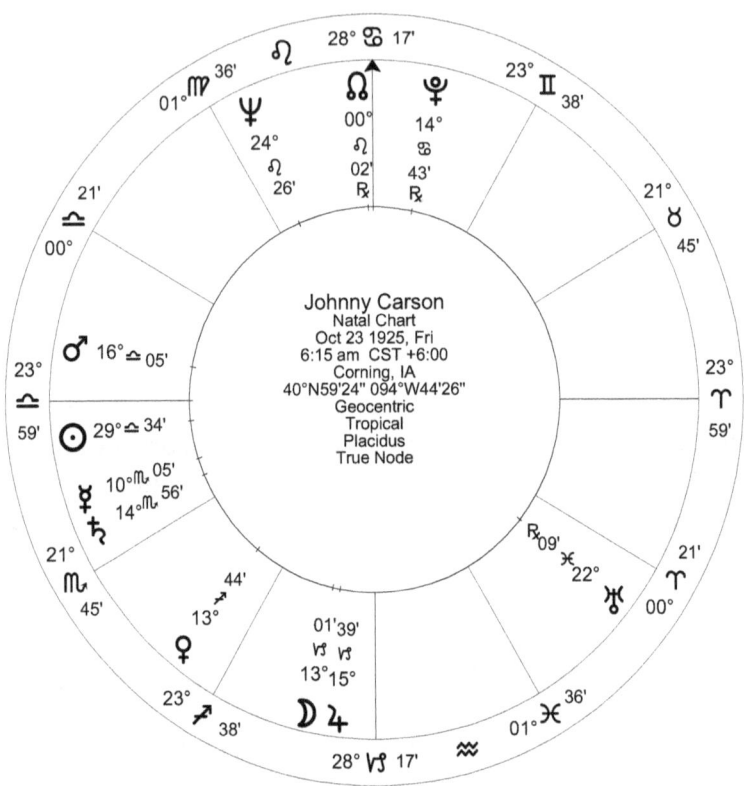

We borrow a key to break open his career interception. A lunar eclipse occurred on April 13, 1945 at 22 Libra 54, within one degree, six minutes of his Ascendant/Descendant. He was married at the time and determined that he was going to work at a radio station. His marriage began going downhill and by the time they had three boys very close in age there was nothing left to repair. Even though he has had a good although rocky career, his home life left much to be desired, or little to be desired and much to be dodged.

In reference to borrowing a key, Aries and Libra are intercepted. Mars rules his work (sixth house) and partners (seventh house) and is in the twelfth in Libra. He chose to play with the women where he worked, and thus destroyed marriages. The key is lost. Venus, ruling the other key, is in the open in the second house. He got his first radio job under an eclipse. The next two eclipses were a lunar at 13 Aries on his Mars and square his Moon, and a solar at 28 Libra, within one-half degree of his Sun. The eclipse immediately prior to *The Tonight Show* was a lunar at 22 Aquarius in his intercepted fourth house. He was not the first host, but he seemed to be destined for the job. *The Tonight Show* moved to California for the sake of convenience and was more to his liking. The lunar eclipse immediately prior to the move was at 9 Leo in his tenth house, and the Sun was at 9 Aquarius.

Johnny Carson's interceptions definitely operated on eclipses. Why are they so prominent in his chart? The Moon rules his tenth house, and Leo, ruled by the Sun, is intercepted in the tenth house. Even though he has the Moon in detriment in Capricorn and in the critical thirteenth degree, it is within two degrees of Jupiter and opposes Pluto at 14 Cancer. This is a powerful configuration if the individual is willing to work at it. He could get his message across. If you look at the Moon's configuration in the third house of wit, you can easily see why his jokes were satirical.

Agatha Christie

Agatha Christie was a prolific novelist who entwined mystery in most of her works. She has Neptune and Pluto, both mystery planets, intercepted in Gemini in the tenth house, and Mars intercepted in the fourth house in Sagittarius. Knowing only that she was a writer who produced books

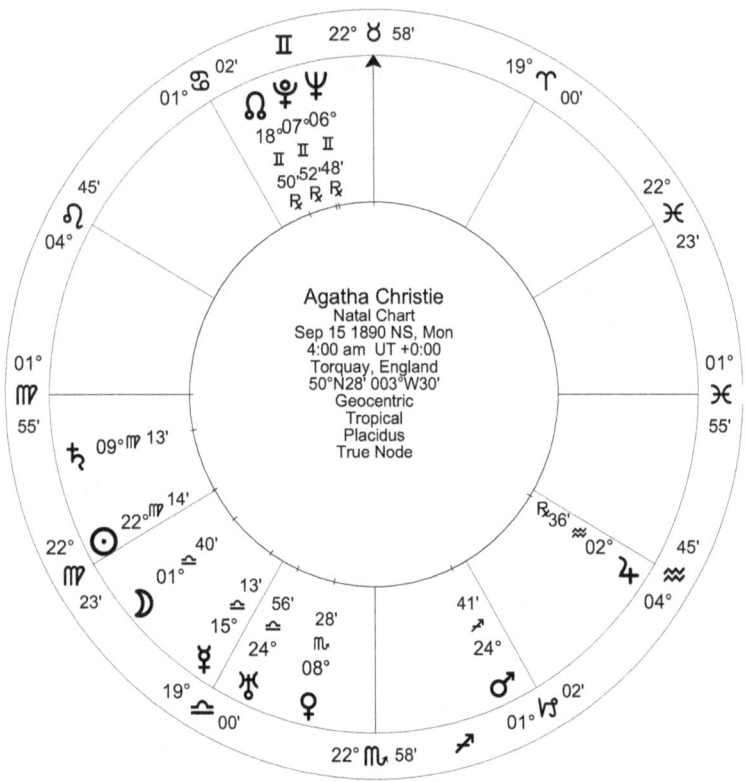

more frequently than some people write letters, my first impression of these planets in intercepted signs was that she wrote to get away from restrictions in her home life. My first inquiry into her more private life revealed that at one point she ran away from home and no one knew where she was for an extended period of time. She learned that her husband *was* involved with another woman and she "went on a trip." She was living in a luxury hotel doing her own thing, writing.

One of her husbands was an archeologist, and she traveled with him and wrote at the sight of the digs. Taylor Caldwell did the same thing, and it later became known that Caldwell seemed to go back in time and, in a trance-like state, viewed the lives of people from the time period being revealed in the dig. Today it is called it channeling.

I would say that the first husband was the one she ran away from because she had Pisces on the seventh house and Neptune square that cusp, which could point to his having a second secret place to hang out. Aries on the ninth house, representing the second husband, and Mars in her fourth house in Sagittarius would point to her traveling with him to their homes away from home.

Helen Blavatsky

Helen Blavatsky founded the Philosophical Society on November 17, 1875, 8:00 p.m., New York, with the assistance of Henry Alcott, a newspaperman. Their first planning meeting was held September 7, 1875 in New York; she had Pluto intercepted in Aries in the tenth house. It is said that one with Pluto in the tenth does something to be remembered after his or her death.

Since she is remembered for the organization she founded, we look at the progressions for that date. She also had Libra intercepted in the fourth house. She was from Russian royalty but stayed in Russia only a short while, and traveled all over the world. She was said to have been in a forced youthful marriage from which she "escaped" after a few months, and has been described as "quite a girl." So much for home life.

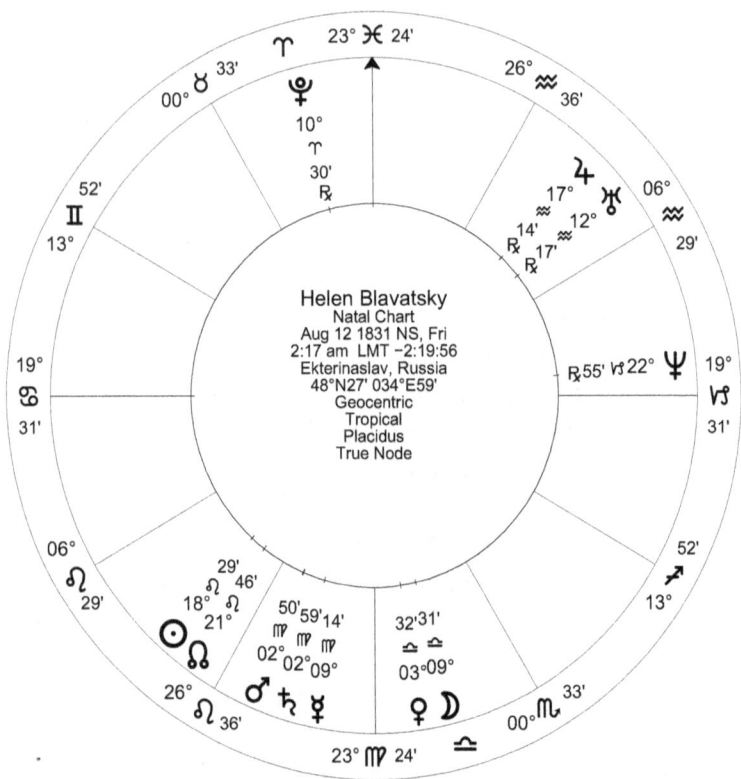

Let's open the tenth house. The keys are Uranus and the Sun and also Saturn because it co-rules Aquarius. On the date of the planning meeting Saturn was conjunct her South Node, possibly a gathering of people from past lives since they had just met when she explained her philosophy to them. Progressed Jupiter was conjunct natal Uranus. All of this was in her eighth house in Aquarius, one of the duplicated signs. The eighth house is significant because it deals with the mysteries of life.

Progressed Sun and progressed Mars were near a conjunction to her natal Venus in the fourth house. By the time that conjunction was exact, she and Henry Alcott left New York and went to India where they organized again.

By the date of the first meeting, November 17, 1875, transiting Saturn was exactly conjunct the progressed South Node and transiting Uranus was exactly conjunct the progressed North Node, only one degree from the natal Sun. The transiting North Node was exactly conjunct progressed Pluto and the transiting South Node was exactly conjunct the natal Moon.

Fifth/Eleventh Houses

This configuration in the natal chart imparts great ability to be creative in new issues. The fifth house supplies the ambition, leadership, pleasure and pride, and the eleventh house indicates original thoughts and the courage to be different by presenting something new and facing new and different people. The eleventh house provides for being a part of an organization without being *the* organization.

Jim Lewis

Jim Lewis, an astrologer, was a person who could go into a new group and make strangers feel as if they had always known him. He was a youthful looking, friendly individual who had a good idea and made it work. He created Astro*Carto*Graphy. Jim had Sagittarius and Gemini intercepted in the fifth and eleventh houses. His duplicated signs were Leo on the first and second houses and Aquarius on the seventh and eighth houses, which can be interpreted as follows:

- Leo on the Ascendant, he needed personal interest; Sun in Gemini in the eleventh, an intellectual interest where friends could be met and cultivated; the Sun is intercepted.
- Leo on the second cusp, something that could bring in money.

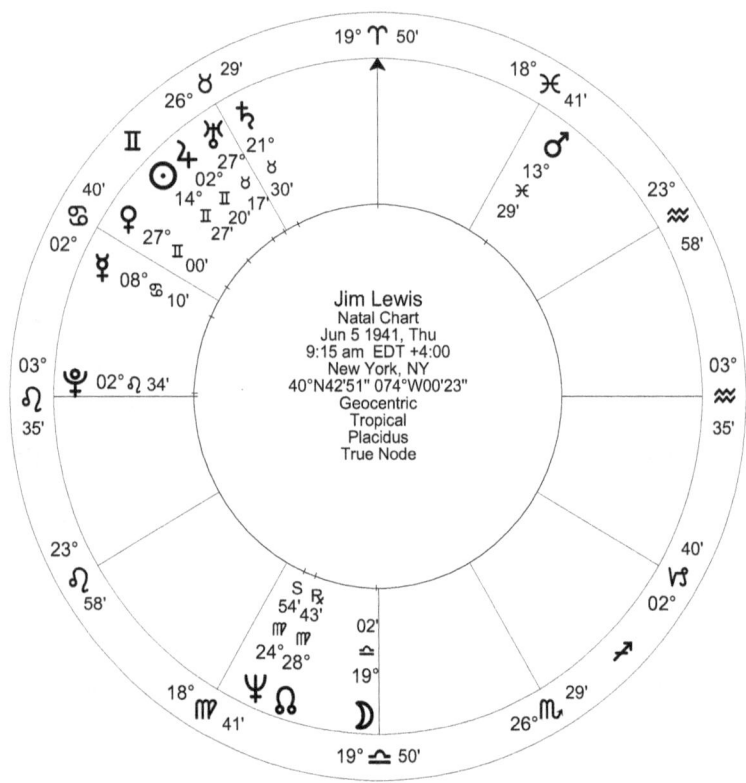

- Aquarius on the seventh house cusp, Uranus in the eleventh, needs someone with whom to share enthusiasm and friendship.
- Aquarius on the eighth house cusp, Uranus in the eleventh in Taurus, not intercepted (a great and handy key), interest should be something unusual and mystical, possibly so unusual it could be a first, or unique, in its application and presentation—the was result *Astro*Carto*Graphy*.

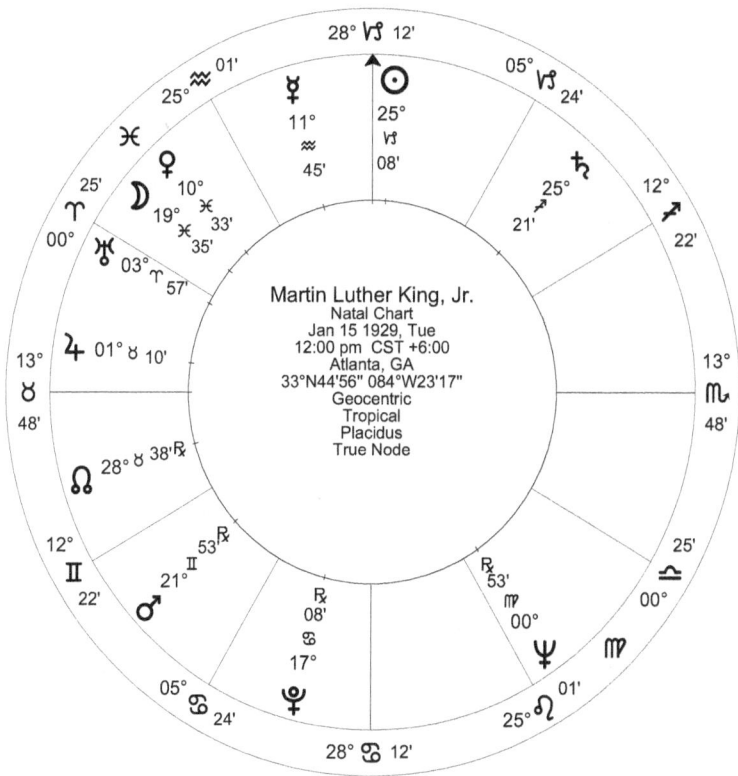

Martin Luther King, Jr.

Civil Rights leader Martin Luther King, Jr. had the Moon and Venus intercepted in the eleventh house in Pisces. He had Neptune in Virgo intercepted in the fifth house. These are appropriate for his goal, "I have a dream." His dream was advanced in process at the time of his death and he had a strong organization to continue to carry out his proposals. How did he unlock the talents he needed for his goal? Cancer and Capricorn are the duplicated signs with the Moon, ruler of Cancer, locked up in the eleventh house. Capricorn was on the cusps of the ninth and tenth houses and Saturn was in Sagittarius in the eighth house.

Martin, an ordained and much loved minister, had an exceptional faith in both God and people. His message was that people could do right and succeed without violence. Yet there were times when a loud minority among a loving, faithful, God-trusting majority would get out of control. Hidden forces were thus working against him. One such took him down on April 4, 1968 in Memphis, Tennessee.

Progressed Saturn was in the degree of his Nodes on the day he led a bus boycott in Montgomery, Alabama, and his progressed Moon, one of the keys, was inside the eleventh house interception in Pisces, exactly half way between natal Venus and natal Moon. Transiting Moon was in his natal third house of communications all day. This was one of the earlier events that he organized over the next thirteen years.

Male Murderer

I do not believe that anyone is destined to be bad. In fact, someone else could have the exact same chart yet use the positive side of its energy and be an enlightened, loving and valuable individual. I believe that following the rules of godliness reaps a different life. This example is to show you a difficult but not impossible chart. Be sure to read the last paragraph for a positive interpretation.

Virgo and Pisces are the intercepted signs in the fifth and eleventh houses with Mars and Neptune in the fifth in Virgo. Leo and Aquarius are the duplicated signs. Leo is on the fourth and fifth houses, and Aquarius occupies the ninth and

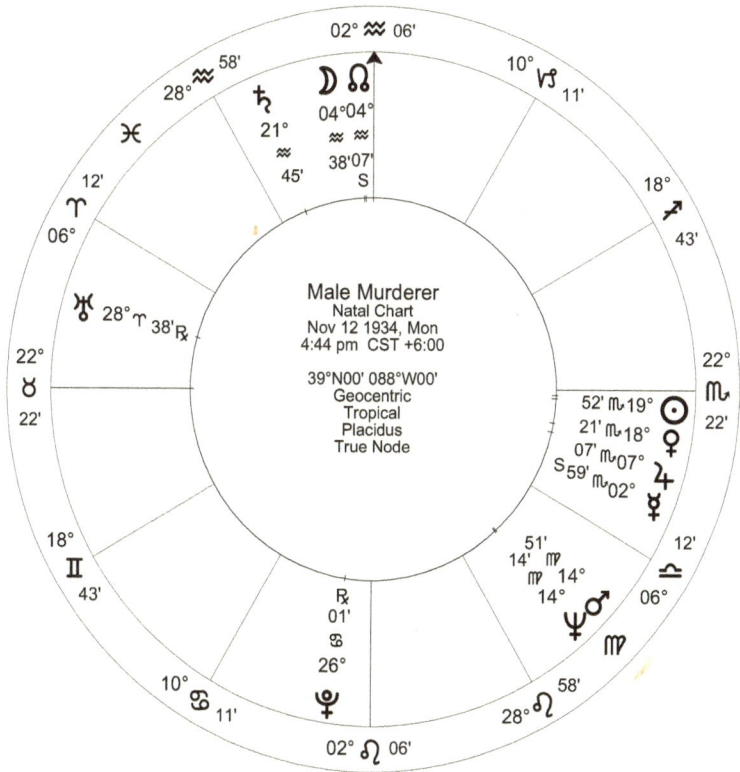

tenth cusps. It is said that "some people insist on getting attention even if it is negative." It seems that this personality was like that. Neptune conjunct Mars in the fifth house will break things and hurt people and then deny it,

Add the interception and more shelter is encouraged. Then put the sign Leo on the cusp and there is an ambition to be a leader, even if into trouble. Neptune being ruled by the opposing sign, Pisces, in the eleventh house of friends organizes friends and drags in more people. The key to the duplicated sign, Leo, is lost in Scorpio in the sixth house conjunct Venus because it can stimulate a love for expressing resentment, hatred and envy. Uranus is the other key, ruling the duplicated sign, Aquarius, but it is hidden in the twelfth and is exactly square Pluto in the third house of the mind. Note that the Sun is in the nineteenth degree "the cursed degree" of the victim or victimizer.

This chart could have been manifested positively in art with Neptune and Mars in the fifth and Pisces totally in the eleventh. Sculpting would have been appropriate, or he could have been a butcher since Virgo rules food preparation. The Sun in Scorpio and other Scorpio planets in the sixth house of service could also belong to a surgical nurse.

This chart could belong to a mathematician, possibly an accountant employed for a unique purpose as indicated by the Moon and Saturn in Aquarius in the tenth. Pluto in the third is persuasive, Mars and Neptune in Virgo can go for idealism, a huddle of Scorpio planets sometimes wants to upgrade the world and the Moon in the tenth appeals to the public. Then allow Chiron to adjust to a higher knowledge and the result could be the best of spiritual leaders.

Sixth/Twelfth Houses

This represents daily routine, service, pets, things that make us sick, the work we do, what we worry about, prayers, life potentials, enemies, fears, what we try to hide, institutions, what is coming up in the future and confinement, whether imposed or by choice. The sixth is the house of work and the twelfth is the house of self-undoing or spiritual evolvement.

William Jennings Bryan

William Jennings Bryan has the most favorable reputation of any consistent loser that can be found. He is classified as an orator, statesman and political leader. He went to law school, graduated and after four years in practice moved to Lincoln, Nebraska, where he became a leading attorney. At age thirty-one he was elected to the U.S. Congress. Solar return Neptune was on his Ascendant. Return Mars was conjunct natal Pluto/Venus in the twelfth house, intercepted in Taurus. Sagittarius and/Gemini were his duplicated signs. Return Mercury was conjunct Neptune. There was no help from Jupiter. He lost his bid for a second term and became editor of the Omaha *World Herald*.

He spoke at the 1898 Democratic convention and won the presidential nomination. Progressed Moon was in his inter-

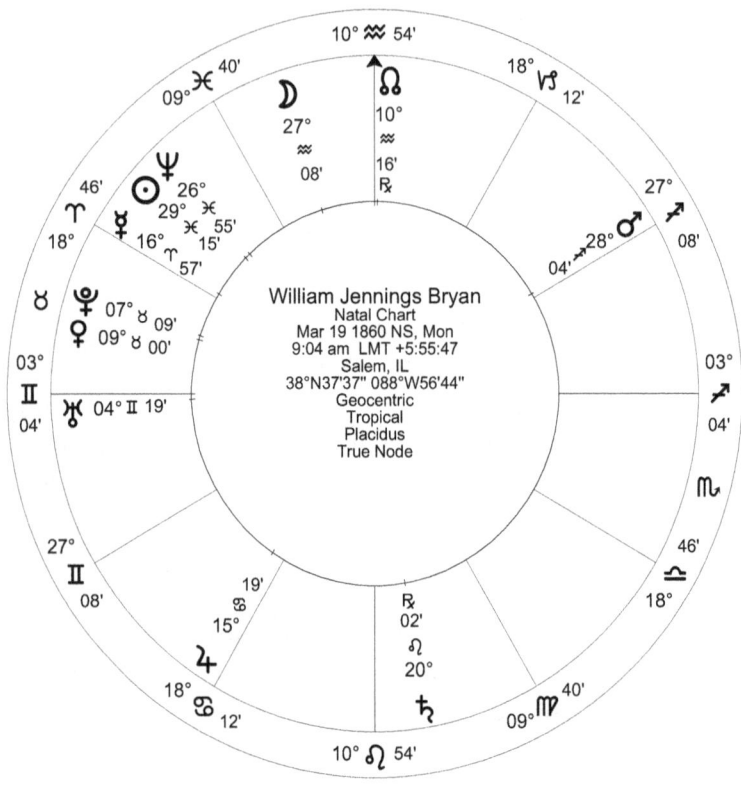

cepted twelfth house. On election day, he lost to William McKinley.

He was chosen as the Democratic nominee in 1908. This time solar return Venus and Mars were intercepted in his natal Taurus twelfth house, Solar return Neptune was conjunct his natal Jupiter (talked so much it couldn't be believed). Return Jupiter was conjunct natal South Node which said "you are an attorney—practice." He lost to William Howard Taft.

He was still noted for the speech of 1896, and was again nominated for president in 1912. The sixth house intercepted sign was Scorpio. Its ruler, Pluto, and co-ruler, Mars, were conjunct in his first house, opposite natal Mars, trine natal Moon and square natal Sun/Neptune conjunction. The force of Pluto and Mars energized him to want to control and resulted in his control of nothing. He lost to Woodrow Wilson.

Bryan was one of the prosecuting attorneys in the John T. Scopes trial that centered on teaching the theory of evolution. The trial was held July 10-21, 1926. Jupiter and Mercury are the keys to the duplicated signs. Transiting Jupiter on July 21 was square natal Mercury and trine progressed Mercury in intercepted Taurus. Transiting Mercury was opposite natal Chiron and Moon and inconjunct natal Neptune/Sun. Transiting Venus and Neptune were conjunct progressed and natal Saturn.

He won the case. Scope was convicted and fined $100, and William Jennings Bryan died in the courtroom. Jupiter and Mercury must have been his escape after all. Venus, ruler of the intercepted twelfth, was conjunct his life enemy, Neptune, and Pluto, ruler of intercepted Scorpio, was conjunct progressed Moon at the critical 13 Cancer. The transiting Sun opposed progressed Mars, co-ruler of Scorpio.

Nikola Tesia

Nikola Tesia, an electrical engineer, was one of the most creative and brilliant inventors of his time. His recognition is low, probably because he invented component parts rather than the whole product. Libra and Aries were intercepted in the sixth and twelfth houses. The duplicated signs were Gemini and Sagittarius.

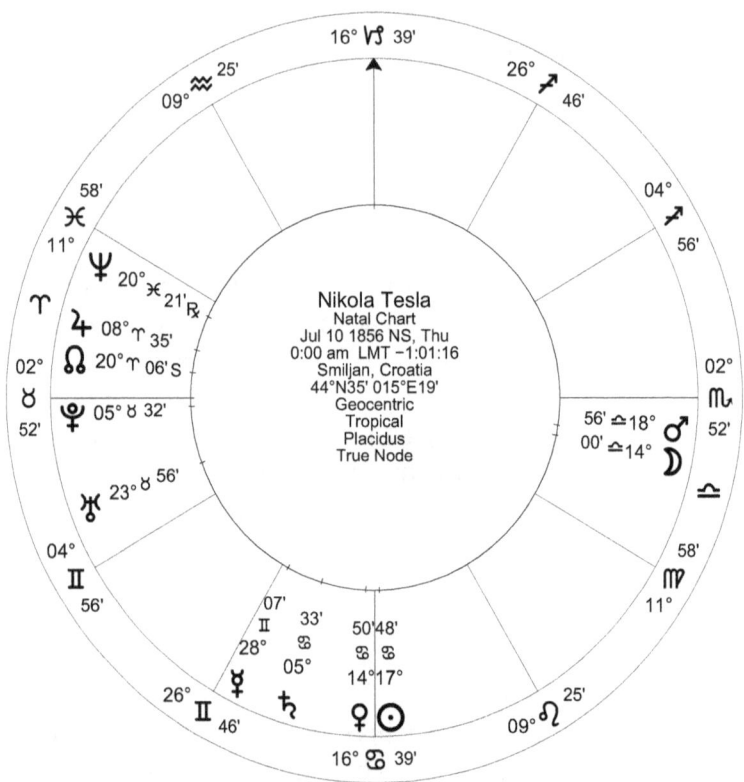

He moved to America in 1884, where he worked with Thomas Edison. His solar return Jupiter was trine natal Jupiter, which was in the intercepted twelfth. This fit a residential change to another continent.

When he should have been working and applying for several inventions in 1888, transiting Jupiter was making a square to progressed Mercury and progressed Venus. Jupiter and Mercury are his keys to unlock the interceptions and Venus rules Libra, the sixth house interception. Venus represents money and it is suspected that his inventions brought some financial benefits, if nothing more than a bonus or royalty from his employer.

During that time Jupiter was also opposing Uranus, which rules electric current and genius. In 1916, solar return Jupiter was on the natal Ascendant and Mercury was at its return to natal Mercury. Both keys were working for him. He received the Edison Medal.

He was able to fulfill Saturn, the tenth house ruler, and Uranus, the house of genius ruler, by perhaps accidentally complying with the planetary energy.

Johnny Cash

Johnny Cash got off drugs and alcohol, was released from prison and met a girl. His interceptions are Pisces in the twelfth house and Virgo in the sixth, with keys Moon and Saturn ruling the duplicated signs. He had a rugged look and a deep voice.

Since drugs were just becoming a subject that could be discussed, he sang about jails and drunks. His Pisces Sun and the ruler of his Ascendant, Mars, and Mercury, which ruled the other intercepted sign, Virgo, were intercepted in Pisces in the twelfth house.

One of the keys, Moon, was in the seventh house. A partner who would mother him would certainly be an asset. Venus rules the seventh house and is in his first. If this mothering woman also loved him, he would be putty in her hands. June Carter was from a close family of gospel singers who

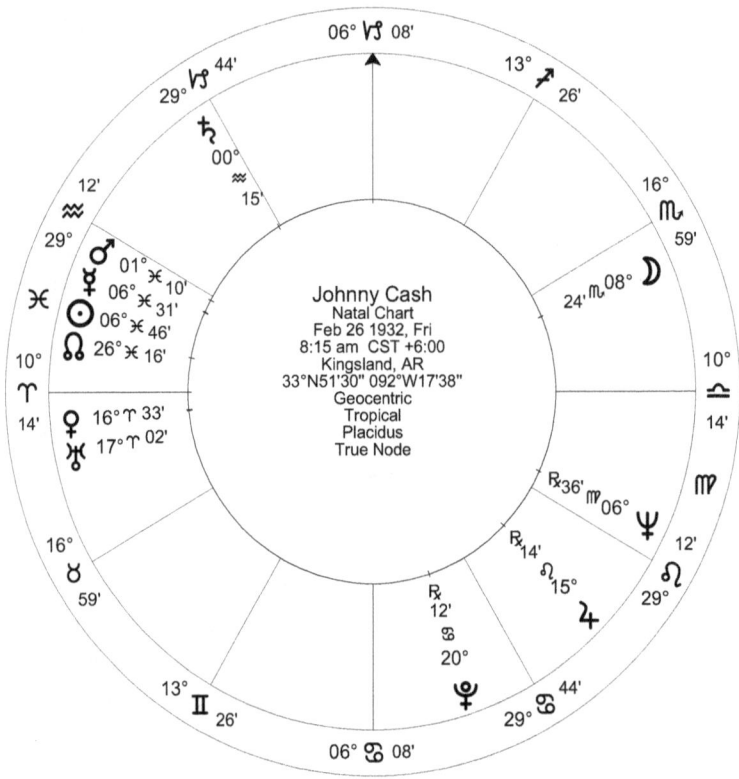

believed in the songs they sang, and her first marriage was crumbling badly. It didn't hurt that she was cute, although not the most beautiful woman on stage. June was a terrific inspiration to Johnny, and he needed all the help he could get to stay sober and straight.

His other key, Saturn, is in the eleventh house at 0 Aquarius. This meant they might have to miss a number of social occasions, but that was okay. June came from a large, loving family and not everybody on the *Grand Ole Opry* was a drinker. It has worked for a number of years. The interceptions may have, in the long run, been experiences that developed into protection.

Multiple Interceptions

It is not unusual to find charts with two sets of interceptions above 50N latitude. Above 60N there might be three or more sets—six signs intercepted. At the Arctic Circle there might be five sets or ten signs intercepted. Once in a while you might find nine signs intercepted; this is a seasonal occurrence.

Be patient when interpreting multiple sets of interceptions. Take each a step at a time, just as you would to interpret several planets in a house, rather than simply saying, "this is where the focus is," or "the focus is in the opposite house." We cannot fully understand an interception by simply looking at the ruler of the sign that is intercepted. The energy in the intercepted signs cannot work openly until it is released.

A solar chart will uphold everything found in a finely tuned chart erected with any house system. If this is not the case, the time of the chart is incorrect. If you are not comfortable with the house placement of any planet in the chart, go back to the solar chart, put the Sun on the Ascendant and see what energies are accented by the planet in question. Then, adjust the chart sufficiently to move the planet into the next closest house and see if the new placement works better.

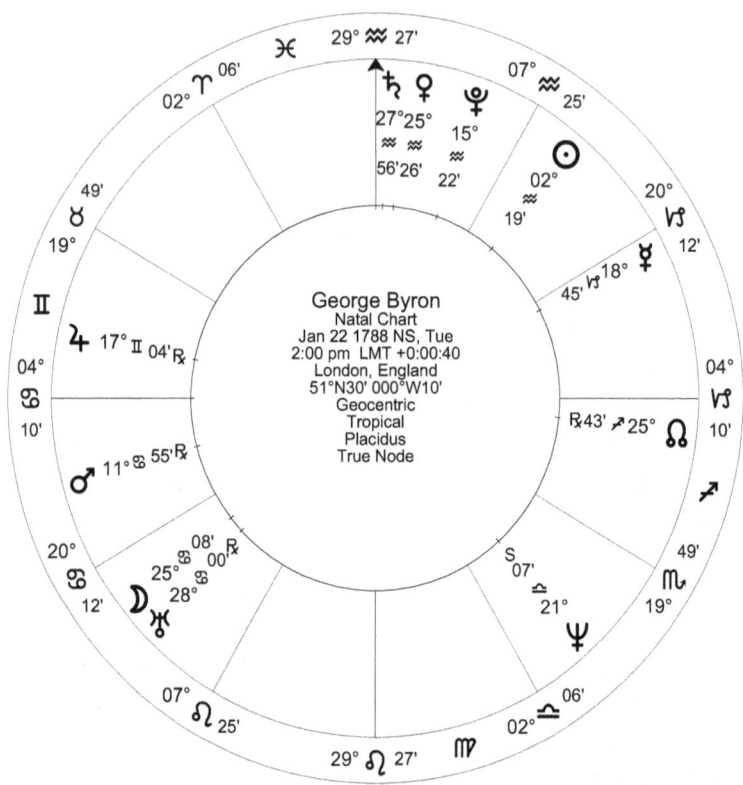

Lord George Gordon Byron

Lord George Gordon Byron had two sets of interceptions. Gemini and Sagittarius were intercepted in the twelfth and sixth houses and Virgo and Pisces were intercepted in the fourth and tenth. His duplicated signs were Cancer, Capricorn, Leo and Aquarius. He unleashed his Jupiter, which was intercepted in the twelfth, through his Moon and Saturn. The Moon in the second house brought him a family inheritance that allowed him to use his time as he pleased, which was writing. Saturn in the ninth in Aquarius allowed him an air of freedom to write openly and, when received by the English, provided him great popularity. Toward the end of his life he left England and his fame subsided. Note that the ruler of the eighth house is in the ninth. He died rather suddenly while away from his homeland.

Lord Byron was born with a club foot. Foot is the twelfth house and, in this case, Taurus, ruled by Venus, with Jupiter intercepted in Gemini. Jupiter is inconjunct Mercury, which rules intercepted Gemini. Venus, twelfth house ruler, is conjunct Saturn in Aquarius sextile the North Node in Sagittarius, and both are inconjunct the Moon and Uranus in Cancer, setting up a karmic yod. The reaction point of the yod is 26 Capricorn 34 in the eighth house. His father died (eighth house) when he was three years old.

When he was eleven, a grand-uncle died and left him an impressive estate. Transiting Saturn, ruler of duplicated Capricorn, was transiting the Moon in the second house. The transiting Nodes were in the sixth and twelfth houses and. The inheritance allowed a move to a more distinguished home and, from all indications, he might well have preferred to have moved alone and left his mother locked up in the tenth house. However, he spent most of his time in private schools where he distinguished himself "by his unsystematic" reading. Transiting Pluto was at 0 Pisces, intercepted in the tenth just blasted open by Pluto.

Byron's first collection of poetry was published just prior to his eighteenth birthday. Progressed Venus, Midheaven and Moon sat squarely on solar return Venus in intercepted Pisces in the tenth house. Progressed Saturn was at 0 Pisces, holding the door open that Pluto had blasted seven years before. Transiting Jupiter had just gone over the North Node in Sagittarius, certainly a good time to publish. The North Node finishes things. These were the poems of his childhood and youth dealing mostly with his love of nature. The next year he published a more adult volume, followed by satire. Uranus was transiting through his intercepted Virgo fourth house.

In 1823, in a passion for liberty, he joined in a struggle for independence for Greece. His progressed Ascendant was conjunct his natal Uranus; Aquarius rules his ninth and tenth houses. His solar return Uranus was in his seventh house of conflict square progressed Venus in Aries and opposite progressed Mars in Cancer. Mercury, ruler of intercepted Gemini and intercepted Virgo, of the solar return was conjunct natal Pluto, providing courage. He became ill while riding in the rain, developed a fever and died April 19, 1824 in Missolonghi, Greece, ten days later. His progressed Sun, ruler of houses three and four, was at 7 Pisces at the same degree of the solar return Nodes on the third and ninth house cusps of the duplicated signs, Leo and Aquarius.

Lord Byron Solar Chart

Our purpose here is to show that the timed chart must tie to the solar chart and that the timed chart gives more details to the original promise of birth. This is why we bother with details. We wish to prove that an astrologer can help someone who knows nothing more than the day, month and year of birth.

As you can see, Lord Byron's solar chart has zero degrees on all house cusps with Aquarius in the position of the As-

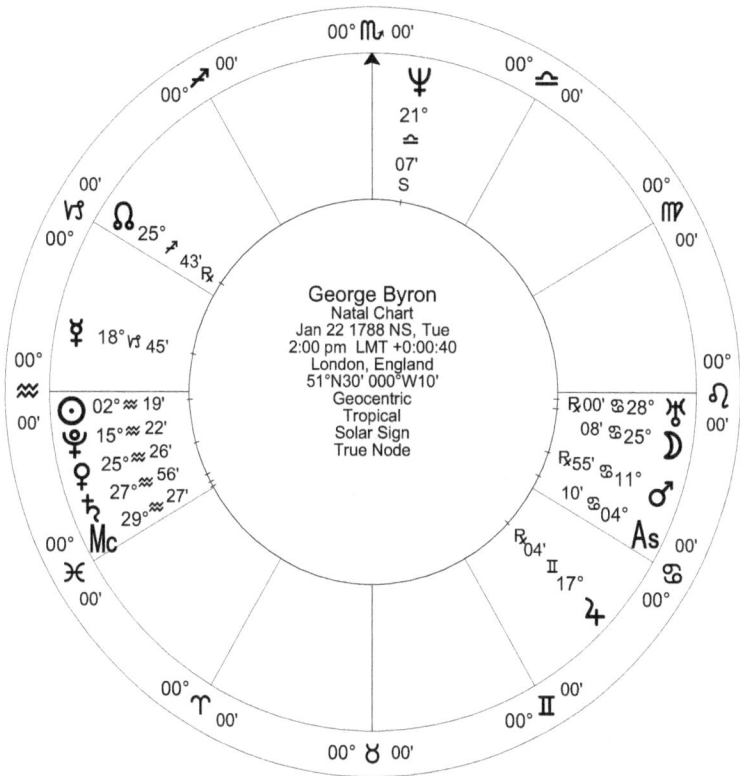

cendant. You also can use the Sun's degree on the Ascendant. The following data shows how the two charts connect (SC = solar chart; TC = timed chart):

SC—Anyone who has the Sun in Aquarius desires to be free and individualistic. Pluto, Venus, and Saturn are in the ninth house. TC—Anyone with Mars in the first house does not ask permission, which was a problem for Byron's mother.

SC—Mars, the Moon and Uranus in Cancer is a very caring person, interested in nature in one's own time. TC—Mars in Cancer in the first house.

SC—Pisces second house signifies that values are spiritual and mystical. Neptune in Libra is artistic and in the ninth house is publishing. Money possibly through a partnership. His father died when he was three. Legal descent would have passed through his father to him. TC—Moon and Uranus in the second. Unexpected money from a family member.

SC—Venus rules the fourth of one of the parents and is besieged (between two malefics) by Pluto (death) and Saturn (father). On the tenth house is Scorpio, representing death, control, sexuality and control of other people's things, which describes his mother. At the rate of one degree per year, Neptune would reach 0 Scorpio about a year short of the time his uncle died. From that time his mother managed his finances. TC—The fourth and tenth houses are intercepted in the timed chart. His father was closed away from him and so was his mother in attitudes because she was too liberal and too strict; he never knew what to expect; Neptune transiting the solar tenth. With this development we could suspect that she enjoyed his inheritance, though to my knowledge there is no mention of it.

SC—Mercury in Capricorn occupied the twelfth solar house of mental disturbance, and was square Neptune in the ninth, indicating the way one walks, trouble with feet (he had one club foot). TC—One of the interceptions was in the twelfth with Jupiter. which is inconjunct Mercury (the mind), Saturn (bones) and Jupiter (walk).

Ten Signs Intercepted in Two Houses

This event, a plane crash involving Wiley Post and Will Rogers, was above 60N latitude and thus cannot be calculated in the Placidus system in astrological software. Wiley Post's watch was broken as a result of the crash and thus recorded the exact time (August 15, 1935, 7:18 p.m., 71N07, 156W24). A man some distance away saw the "bird go down" and, knowing that there was nothing he could do for anyone, immediately went for help. It took him three and a half hours to reach the U.S. Army Signal Corps station. Sergeant Morgan rounded up a crew of Eskimo seal hunters and returned to the crash site as quickly as possible. The site was reached seven hours and twelve minutes after the crash. It was determined that both had died instantly.

In a hand-calculated chart (not shown) it appears that every planet is intercepted, but Uranus is in Taurus (not intercepted) and Jupiter and Mars are in Scorpio in the eighth house (not intercepted). Uranus represents the friend of humanity and the people who returned with him to the scene. Jupiter is always in some important position in a death chart, and here is in Scorpio and in the eighth house. Mars is the only one of the three that is a key to open the interceptions. It co-rules Scorpio. Mars has special significance according to the following from *Celestial SuperRulers*:

"Mars in Scorpio or the eighth house represents not unbridled activity but sheer power. No popping firecracker here, we're talking nuclear bombs. When this one is around you are aware of him because of his intensity and air of being in control. He may be the strong, silent type, one who plans every action and anticipates each reaction, or he can be manipulative, sarcastic and perhaps abusive but, one way or another, he will get things done.

"When Mars is in Scorpio and Pluto is in a water sign, there is a danger of the native becoming mentally imbalanced or totally 'unglued,' but there is a far better possibility for the person to be creative, intuitive, imaginative and even psychic. Here we have gifted and dramatic actors, graceful and powerful dancers or forceful and dynamic leaders. These individuals instinctively know when to be where and what to do at the time they get there. This is the angel who shows up and grabs you before you fall off the cliff or pulls his boat alongside and throws you a life jacket just as you're on your way down for the third time."

There was no one else. All planets but three are intercepted. When the angel went for help. it was deathly silent. Enough said.

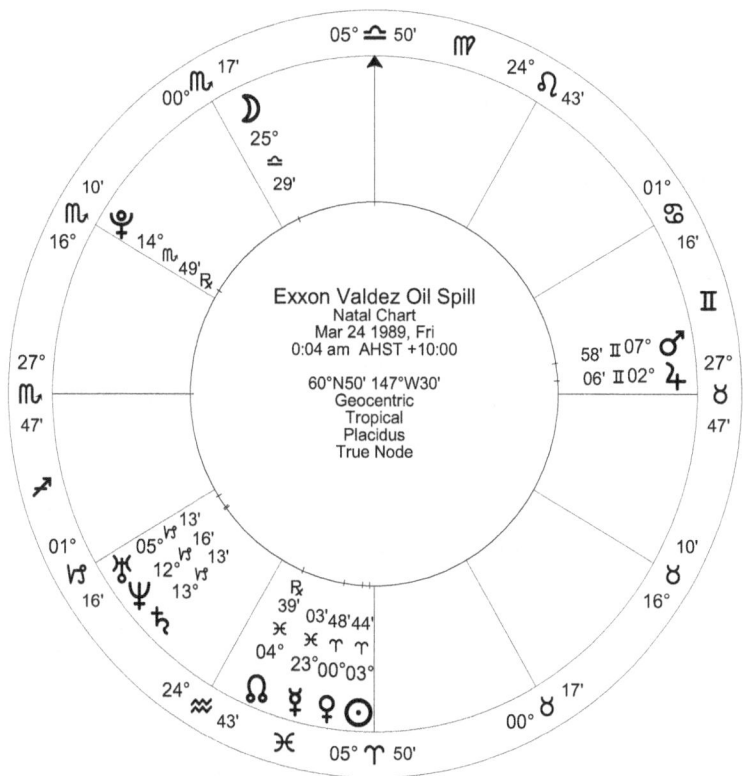

Exxon Valdez Alaskan Oil Spill

This event occurred at a time when I was not the least interested in current events outside of my personal circle, family, friends, clients, students and daily contacts.

When I first looked at the chart of this event I knew nothing of the circumstances. Knowing only that it was an oil spill, I looked immediately to the tenth house to see if there was neglect on the part of the authority figure. The Moon (emotions) in the tenth house rules the eighth (no comment at this point). The Moon is in Libra, ruled by Venus, as is the Midheaven. Venus is in Aries, the third house, but not in the interception. Venus is the authority figure. It appears that the authority had a message but was involved in something personal and did not respond. Venus at 0 Aries says, "I'm having fun and will take care of that in my own time."

What about the message? Mercury rules messages and both Gemini in the seventh house and Virgo in the ninth house are intercepted. Mercury is also intercepted in Pisces in the third house. This is another endorsement that the message is ignored. The chart also shows great financial loss. The Ascendant of the chart is the event; consequently, the second house represents its value. Uranus is the first planet, the sudden event, and inconjunct both Jupiter and Mars in the seventh house in Gemini–episodes that are out of control. Neptune is the second planet ruler of Pisces and co-ruler of Sagittarius, and both signs are intercepted. Neptune is oil not available. Saturn is in the critical thirteenth degree of Capricorn ruling the second house and co-ruling the third, indicating major decisions concerning the losses and paperwork related to the event. To show the complexity of the event, the Moon is void of course.

This chart is ruled by Scorpio, so what does Pluto tell us? There are three houses ruled by Scorpio, and Pluto occupies the eleventh. We have already identified the tenth house of this event as being the person in charge. The eleventh house then represents that person's money and values. Pluto can be big income or a sizable wipe out. Some would say that there is a trine to Mercury, but Mercury moves much faster than Pluto and Mercury has passed that aspect. The only aspects to Pluto are the sextiles from very slow moving Uranus, Neptune and Saturn, so my guess is that the best the boss could get out of it was the good fortune to keep his life. The Moon was void of course.

How did the rulers of the two duplicated signs perform to open the interceptions? The messenger, or employee, who delivered the message was persistent and did get through. The message was ignored or acted upon too late.

Pluto is the ruler and Mars the co-ruler of the other duplicated sign, Scorpio. Mars in Gemini is the message, already discussed. Pluto, the great power, is retrograde and could do nothing more than use the Capricorn sextile to recoup whatever losses possible.

This event is like the lives of too many insensitive people who ignore the universal warnings. Each of us is a part of the whole and when we ignore all but our own selfish desires we find in the end we too may have to "pay more for oil spill products."

More on Interceptions

Interceptions in the natal chart will change by progression. Due to signs of long and short ascension it is not practical for me to work out a scale for knowing how long it will take to progress out of interceptions. As for interpretations, you might want to try what is proposed here or stay with the old system of looking at the ruler of the intercepted sign and the houses of the interceptions only. You won't learn much, but it's better than nothing. This could be compared with going home and finding you lost your door key. You look at the house and decide you are at the correct address but you can't get in. And you just sit there.

For these studies the natal chart is in the center circle, the progressed chart in the next circle and the date of the event or solar return in the outside circle.

Horary Charts with Interceptions

An interception in the horary chart might indicate that some event is on hold or delayed. It might mean that something or someone is closed out or closed in, as if confined. An item might be in a box, in a closet, in a drawer or in a pocket. Sometimes something or someone represented by an intercepted sign received protection. Interceptions do not necessarily mean that things or people are gone forever.

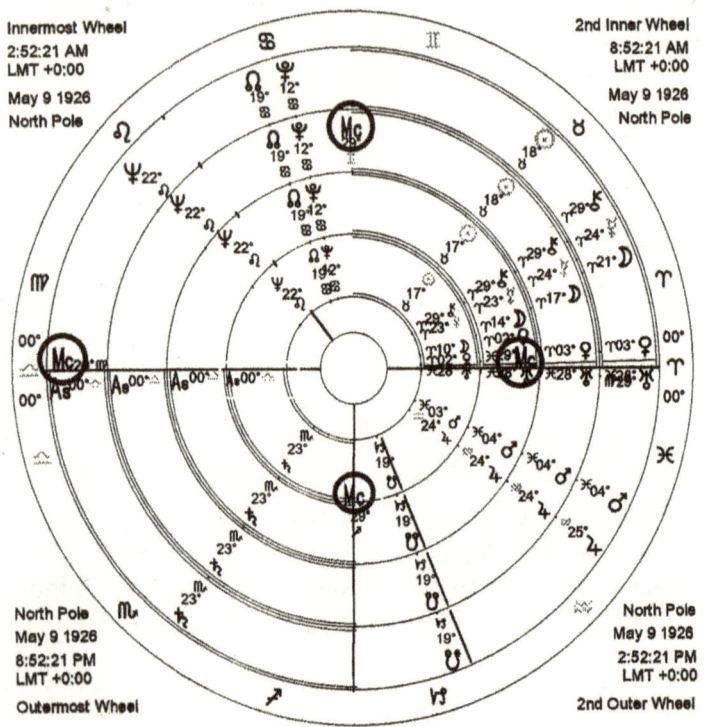

Interesting Interception Charts

The chart shown here demonstrates the position of the Midheaven at the North Pole during a sequence of four different times on the same date: 02:52:21 (innermost wheel), 08:52:21 (second inner wheel), 14:52:21 (second outer wheel) and 20:52:21 (outermost wheel). They are for May 9, 1926; 90N00, 00W00, Tropical, Regiomontanus house system, LMT times. Notice how the Midheaven moves all around the chart but the Sun does not change its position significantly and the Ascendant remains at the same degree on all four charts. This is because:

- The Midheaven in this house system is not the tenth house cusp, as in Placidus and Koch.
- The houses are proportional and not equal and, because of multiple interceptions the charts, "fill up the space," as it were, in the large houses while some houses might occupy a sliver and be only a few degrees or even minutes wide.
- The Ascendant remains on the western horizon at its normal position because at the very top of Earth you can see forever. There is no horizon, and therefore the Ascendant stays the same for long periods of time.

When reviewing charts cast for extreme northern and southern latitudes, remember that in the summer the north polar regions are called "the land of the midnight sun," while in the winter it stays dark for days at a time.

In the second example we have a set of interesting interception charts. There are four different charts drawn for the same time of day on each of the cardinal ingresses. Each chart is cast using Tropical Regiomontanus with midnight as the time (it works the same if noon or any other consistent time is used). All charts are cast at the coordinates: 090N00, 00W00.

Chart 2-A is cast for December 22, 1996, Chart 2-B is cast for March 21,1996, Chart 2-C is cast for June 22,1996 and Chart 2-D is cast for September 23,1996.

Note how the Sun moves into each of the angles as the seasons change. Chart 2-A shows the Sun in the bottom of the chart at 0 Capricorn; Chart 2-B shows the Sun at the Descendant (west) side of the chart at 0 Aries; Chart 2-C shows the

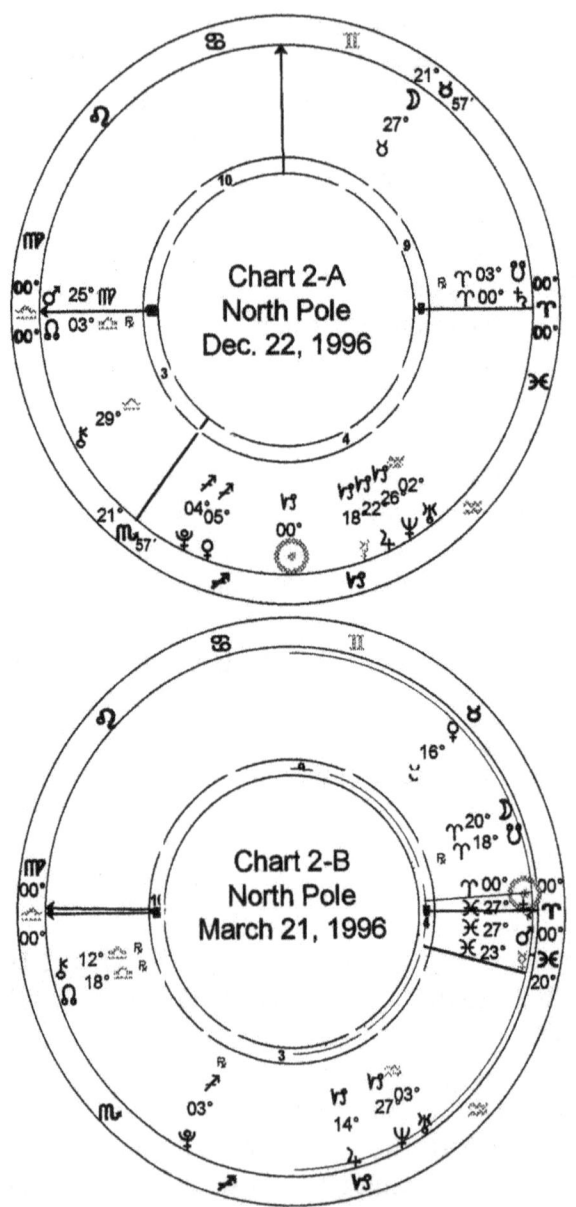

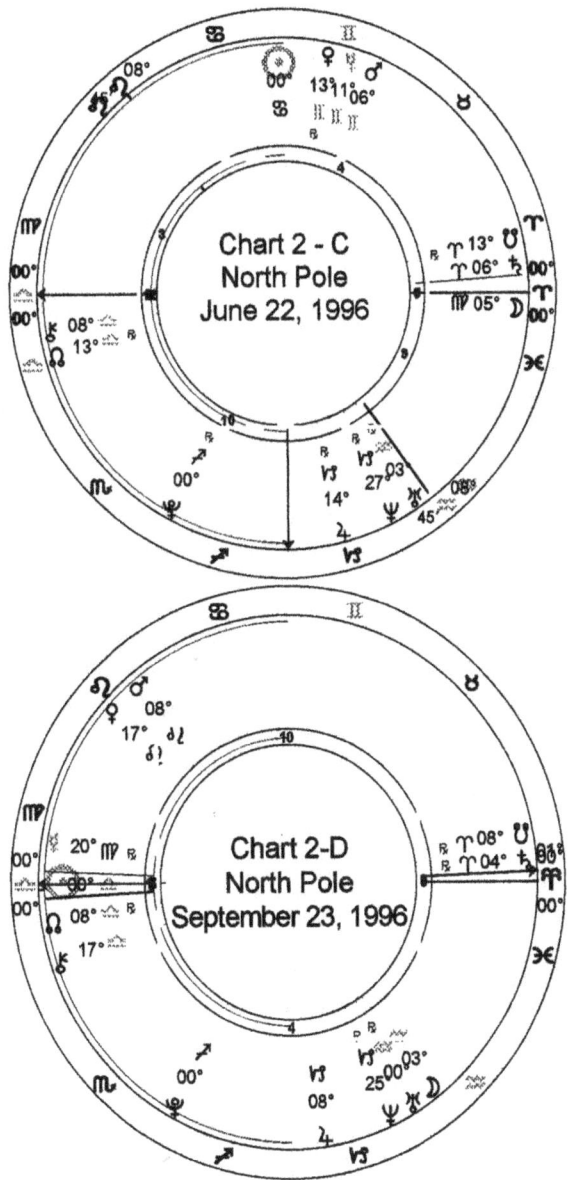

Sun in the top of the chart at 0 Cancer; and Chart 2-D shows the Sun at the Ascendant (east) of the chart at 0 Libra.

The last set of charts is cast for Port Radium, Canada, 66N06, 118W030. All charts are cast using Tropical Placidus, not-proportional houses, PST, December 23, 1996.

If you look at all of the charts as the time of the day changes from midnight through the day and back to midnight again, the Sun gradually travels from the bottom of the chart around to the Ascendant. From the Ascendant, the Sun jumps over to the eastern side of the chart from 11:00 a.m. to 1:00 p.m. and then travels gradually around to its starting point.

If a series of charts were to be cast for every other odd hour to show the progress of the Sun, the following would be noted:

1:00 a.m., Sun in third, near fourth cusp at 1 Capricorn
3:00 a.m., Sun in third, near third cusp at 1 Capricorn
5:00 a.m., Sun in second, near middle at 1 Capricorn
7:00 a.m., Sun in second, near second cusp at 2 Capricorn
9:00 a.m., Sun in first, near middle at 2 Capricorn
11:00 a.m., Sun in first, near Ascendant at 2 Capricorn
Noon, Sun moves from Ascendant to Descendant
1:00 p.m., Sun in sixth, near Descendant at 2 Capricorn
3:00 p.m., Sun in sixth, near middle at 2 Capricorn
5:00 p.m., Sun in fifth, near sixth cusp at 2 Capricorn
7:00 p.m., Sun in fifth, near middle at 2 Capricorn
9:00 p.m., Sun in fourth, near middle at 2 Capricorn
11:00 p.m., Sun in fourth, near fourth cusp at 2 Capricorn

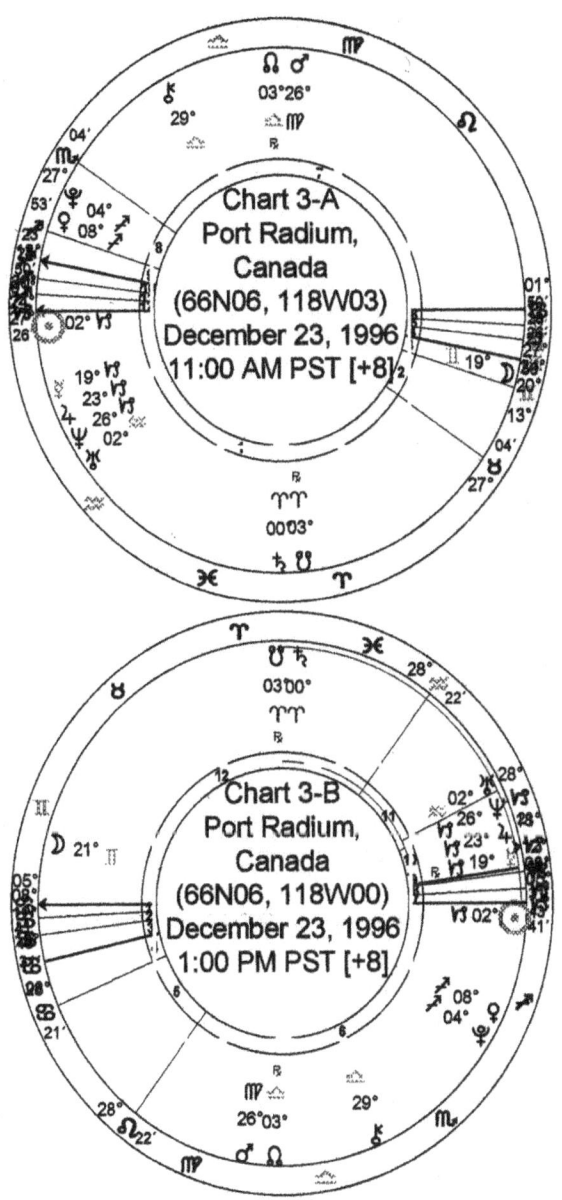

To illustrate the movement of the Sun from the Ascendant side at 11:00 a.m. to the Descendant side at 1:00 p.m., charts for these two times are shown (Charts 3-A and 3-B).

Summary of Interpretation Method

When working with interpretations you should not approach it as, *"The interceptions are in the third and ninth houses. You have to work hard at communications. The signs are Virgo and Pisces and you don't communicate well."* This is obviously of absolutely no use in helping the individual understand the difficulties he or she might experience, for example, in communication or, in this specific instance, what might be encountered with respect to personal work and pleasure time, all of which might be destroyed by sympathy seekers, who can be represented by the interceptions.

Throughout this book there are interpretations of real people's charts. Reading the examples will reveal different avenues of unlocking under varying circumstances, most of which just normally happen if we simply live in the most wholesome manner.

Step 1

Identify the houses holding the interceptions and recognize the departments of life affected by the interceptions. If there is one set of interceptions, identify both houses. If there are five sets, identify all ten, one set at a time. With more than two it might be easier to work backward using the signs and planets not intercepted.

Step 2

Identify the duplicated signs (signs on more than one house cusp). Are their rulers in open signs or in intercepted signs? These planets are the keys that will open the interceptions. If any are in intercepted signs, the energy will not be easily accessible. If all the keys are locked up, it might not be easy. In fact, the individual might decide to let sleeping dogs lie rather than try to awaken them.

Step 3

Locate the rulers of the intercepted signs. If they are inside the interception, they are SuperRulers. A planet in the sign it rules is dignified, has special power and might be able to blast open the locked box from the inside. For more information on SuperRulers, see *Celestial SuperRulers* by Diane and Rudy Flack. If the ruler is out of the interception, it might be in the sign of its co-ruler, which gives it strength, or it might have a beneficial aspect to some other planet.

Step 4

For more assistance or explanation on unlocking the interceptions, watch for transits that enter the intercepted signs and conjunctions to the ruler of the signs.

Step 5

Progressions are slow travelers that come to visit for a long time and open a high percentage of interceptions.

Step 6

Another potential key might be an eclipse bombarding the intercepted sign. It's hard to stay in a house when lightening strikes it. We might think of an eclipse opening an interception as being unlocked by a borrowed key. The Nodes opening interceptions will open from the back door because they back in. Retrograde planets by progression may also unlock the back door of an interception to open it.

Step 7

We have not dealt with declinations in this book but they too can open interceptions. Interceptions and declinations are extremely indicative of karma and are involved in some of the most important actions and non-actions of our lives.

Step 8

In this material we have not dwelt upon the rulers of the signs on the cusps of the houses holding the interceptions. It seems entirely correct to consider the ruler on the cusp to represent a symbol of the door knob or escape hatch. For example, Mother Teresa had interceptions in the fourth and tenth houses. Scorpio ruled the fourth house and Pluto was in the tenth. Her father's death when she was ten strongly affected her life. Venus ruled her tenth house with Gemini intercepted; Venus was in her twelfth house. The love of her life was commitment to total poverty.

Step 9

Use your imagination when interpreting anything. Try it, you won't break it.